IROQUOIS

Big Buddy Books
An Imprint of Abdo Publishing
www.abdopublishing.com

Sarah Tieck

www.abdopublishing.com

Published by Abdo Publishing, a division of ABDO, PO Box 398166, Minneapolis, Minnesota 55439.
Copyright © 2015 by Abdo Consulting Group, Inc. International copyrights reserved in all countries. No part
of this book may be reproduced in any form without written permission from the publisher. Big Buddy Books™
is a trademark and logo of Abdo Publishing.

Printed in the United States of America, North Mankato, Minnesota.
052014
092014

Cover Photo: © Nathan Benn/Alamy.
Interior Photos: ASSOCIATED PRESS (p. 27); Getty Images (pp. 23, 30); © NativeStock.com/AngelWynn (pp. 9, 13,
    15, 16, 17, 21, 26); North Wind Picture Archives (p. 25); © Photoshot Holdings Ltd/Alamy (p. 5); © Philip Scalia/
    Alamy (p. 29); Shutterstock (pp. 11, 19).

Coordinating Series Editor: Rochelle Baltzer
Contributing Editors: Bridget O'Brien, Marcia Zappa
Graphic Design: Adam Craven

Library of Congress Cataloging-in-Publication Data

Tieck, Sarah, 1976-
  Iroquois / Sarah Tieck.
      pages cm. -- (Native Americans)
  ISBN 978-1-62403-354-4
  1. Iroquois Indians--Juvenile literature. I. Title.
  E99.I7T54 2015
  974.7004'9755--dc23
                                2014005984

CONTENTS

Amazing People

Hundreds of years ago, North America was mostly wild, open land. Native Americans lived there. They had their own languages and **customs**.

The Iroquois (IHR-uh-kwoy) are a Native American group. They are known for having a well-organized government and skilled fighters. Let's learn more about these Native Americans.

Did You Know?

People looked to the Iroquois system of government when forming the US government.

The name *Iroquois* means "rattlesnakes." It came from a French form of an Algonquian word.

IROQUOIS TERRITORY

Iroquois homelands were in the northeast. The area included parts of present-day New York, Pennsylvania, and Canada. Land in the northeast has mountains, coasts, farmlands, and forests. Some of the Great Lakes are nearby. There was a rich fur trade in the area.

The Iroquois were known as the Five Nations. By about 1600, the Mohawk, Onondaga, Cayuga, Oneida, and Seneca had formed this group. In 1722, the Tuscarora joined to form the Six Nations. These tribes worked together to have a very organized government.

CANADA

UNITED STATES

MEXICO

IROQUOIS HOMELANDS

QUEBEC

MAINE

ONTARIO

VERMONT

NEW HAMPSHIRE

NEW YORK

MASSACHUSETTS

RHODE ISLAND
CONNECTICUT

PENNSYLVANIA

N
W E
S

7

HOME LIFE

The Iroquois lived in longhouses. Longhouses were narrow. They had one room split into parts. They were made with tree branches. The roof was often rounded.

A longhouse was large. Up to 50 people could live in it! Each family had its own small space for sleeping and living. They shared a fire and other parts of the building.

Did You Know?

The Iroquois often called themselves *Haudenosaunee*. This means "the people of the longhouse."

8

Longhouses had doors on each end, but no windows. There were holes in the roof to allow smoke to escape. But otherwise, no other light could come in.

9

What They Ate

The Iroquois were hunters, gatherers, and farmers. The men hunted animals such as deer. They fished using nets and spears. The people also gathered wild fruits, nuts, mushrooms, and roots. The women farmed corn, beans, and squash. If food wasn't available, the Iroquois moved to find it.

Corn (*above*), beans (*left*), and squash (*below*) were known as "the three sisters." They grew well together. Beans grew along corn stalks, and squash spread out around them.

DAILY LIFE

Longhouses were the heart of life in an Iroquois village. Each village usually had several hundred people. Within the village, people had important jobs. Men hunted, fished, and trapped. They were warriors or tribe leaders. They also built houses.

Women planned and cared for the crops. They made clothing. They also chose tribe leaders. Children did chores and played with cornhusk dolls. Boys and men played lacrosse.

Did You Know?

Iroquois women chose the members of the tribal council. They took them out of power if there were problems.

 In the late 1700s, Iroquois men wore long shirts, leather leggings, and silver jewelry.

STRONG FIGHTERS

Iroquois men were strong fighters. Being powerful was important to them. Early on, Iroquois tribes often attacked each other. Many times, they wanted **revenge** for wrongdoing.

The Iroquois harmed or killed many enemies, but they also took **captives**. Some captives were made to work for a tribe. Sometimes, they joined the tribe.

Today, some people wear traditional Iroquois warrior face paint for special events. The colors have special meanings.

MADE BY HAND

The Iroquois made many objects by hand. They used animal bones and skins to make tools, clothes, and other useful objects. They added beauty to everyday life through their arts and crafts.

Beadwork
The Iroquois used colorful beads and porcupine quills to decorate their clothes. They made beaded belts and pouches (*right*). Wampum belts were sewn with purple and white shell beads.

Water Drums

Iroquois music included flute and drum sounds. The drums were filled with water and known for their unusual sounds.

Headdresses

Iroquois men wore feathered caps called *gustowehs*. These showed which tribe each man belonged to. Women sometimes wore beaded headbands.

Lacrosse sticks

The Iroquois played lacrosse with wooden sticks. These were carved from tree branches. The netting was made of animal parts, such as leather.

SPIRIT LIFE

Religion was important to the Iroquois. They believed that life on earth began when a woman fell from the sky. Their religion also included stories about the stars and trips to the otherworld.

The Iroquois had special **rituals** and **ceremonies**. These were important parts of Iroquois life. They also included prayers of thanks. Some honored government events such as **treaty** making.

The Midwinter Ceremony honors new beginnings. It takes place in January or February.

19

STORYTELLERS

Long ago, the Iroquois had no written words. So, they told stories to teach people their history. The stories also shared ideas about their way of life and **traditions**.

Storytellers could help brighten up cold and dark days. A storyteller might carry a bag filled with objects. He or she would pull an object from the bag and tell a story related to it. Stories were sometimes told at the beginning of **ceremonies** and **rituals**.

Iroquois storytellers often used music to make their stories come alive for others.

FIGHTING FOR LAND

Land was important to the Iroquois. According to one story, the five major Iroquois tribes fought each other for many years. They fought to **protect** their land and families and to gain power.

In the 1500s, Hiawatha and Deganawidah, or the Peacemaker, helped the tribes make peace. This is how the Mohawk, Oneida, Onondaga, Seneca, and Cayuga came together.

"From his forehead fell
his tresses,
Smooth and parted like
a woman's."

"The Song of Hiawatha."
—*Longfellow.*

 In 1855, a poem was printed about Hiawatha's life. It was called *The Song of Hiawatha*, by Henry Wadsworth Longfellow.

Working together, the Iroquois grew very powerful. In the 1600s, they got guns from Dutch settlers. After that, they gained power over other nearby tribes. They hunted and traded furs. They also controlled the boats in the Great Lakes.

Beginning in the mid-1800s, the US and Canadian governments made the Iroquois live on **reservations**. Some Iroquois moved, but a large group resisted moving from their homelands. Today, they live in Canada, Wisconsin, Oklahoma, and New York. They use laws to **protect** their land and rights.

The Iroquois joined the Dutch and the English to fight the French and other Native American nations.

BACK IN TIME

By about 1600

The five major Iroquois tribes had formed what would be called the Five Nations.

1500s

Hiawatha and Deganawidah visited the Mohawk, Oneida, Onondaga, Seneca, and Cayuga. These men worked to help them make peace.

1722

The Tuscarora joined the Iroquois League. It was then called the Six Nations.

1983

The Iroquois Nationals lacrosse team formed. The tribes had been playing this game since the 1600s. Today, the team plays around the world.

1775

The Revolutionary War began in America. The Oneida and Tuscarora fought with the American colonists. The other Iroquois tribes fought with the British. The war ended in 1783.

2010

The US government counted about 40,000 Iroquois living in the United States.

STRONG NATIONS

The Iroquois people have a long, rich history. They are remembered for building a strong group of nations. They are also known for their longhouses and the game of lacrosse.

Iroquois roots run deep. Today, the people have kept alive those special things that make them Iroquois. Even though times have changed, many people carry the **traditions**, stories, and memories of the past into the present.

Today, the Iroquois come
together to honor traditions.

"Let us survive

Inside a sacred space.

Look at the Earth.

She feels us. She feeds us."

— Roberta Hill Whiteman

GLOSSARY

captive someone who is held as a prisoner or locked up.

ceremony a formal event on a special occasion.

custom a practice that has been around a long time and is common to a group or a place.

protect (pruh-TEHKT) to guard against harm or danger.

reservation (reh-zuhr-VAY-shuhn) a piece of land set aside by the government for Native Americans to live on.

revenge the act of hurting someone for an injury or wrong that was suffered.

ritual (RIH-chuh-wuhl) a formal act or set of acts that is repeated.

tradition (truh-DIH-shuhn) a belief, a custom, or a story handed down from older people to younger people.

treaty an agreement made between two or more groups.

WEBSITES

To learn more about Native Americans, visit **booklinks.abdopublishing.com**. These links are routinely monitored and updated to provide the most current information available.

INDEX